PIANO SOLOS

T0058957

7777 W. BLUEMOUND RD. P.O. BOX 13819 MILWAUKEE, WI 53213

Richard Clayderman plays Love Songs of the World

AUTUMN LEAVES
(LES FEUILLES MORTES)

English Lyric by
JOHNNY MERCER
French Lyric by
JACQUES PREVERT

Music by
JOSEPH KOSMA
Arranged by GEORGE H. GREELEY

Con Espressione

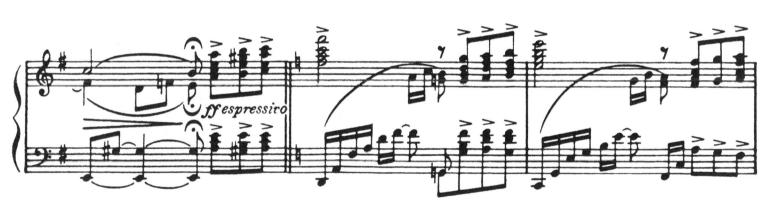

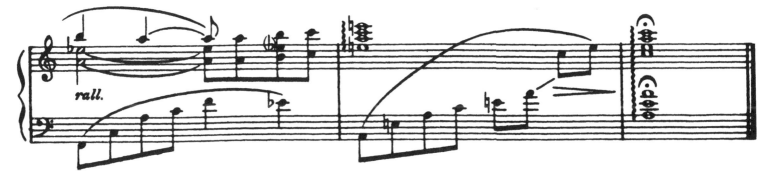

CARA MIA

Words and Music by TULIO TRAPANI
and LEE LANGE
Arranged by DICK AVERRE

Slowly and expressively

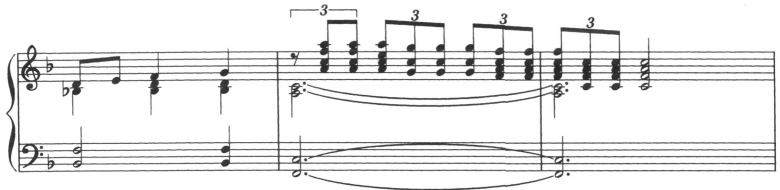

In a flowing style

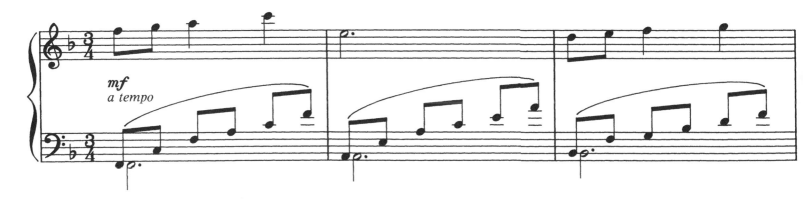

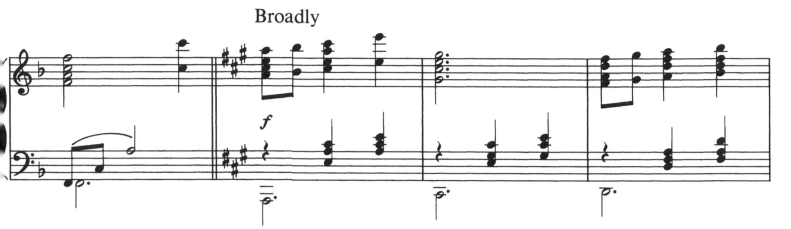

Broadly

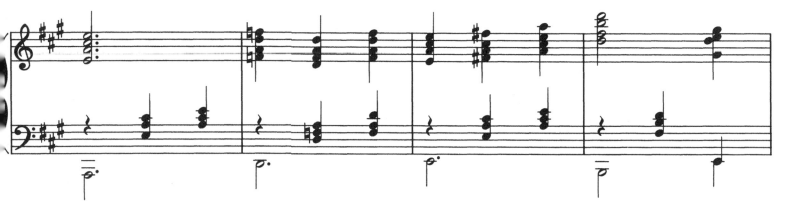

Vigorously

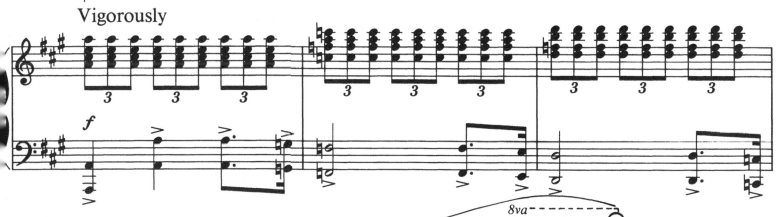

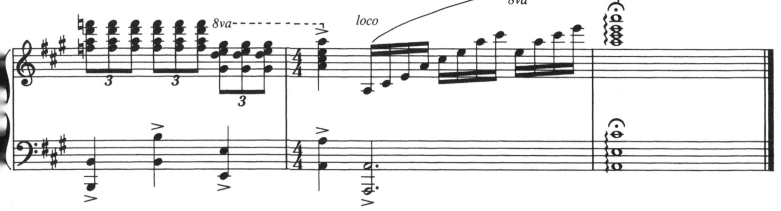

FRAGILE HEART

Music by PAUL de SENNEVILLE
and JEAN BAUDLOT
Arranged by DICK AVERRE

Freely

In a slow flowing tempo

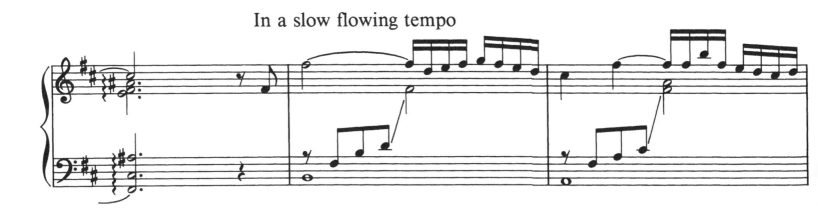

Freely

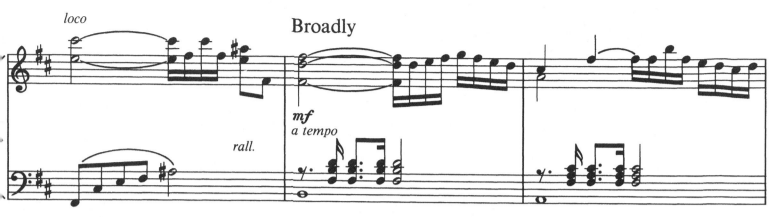

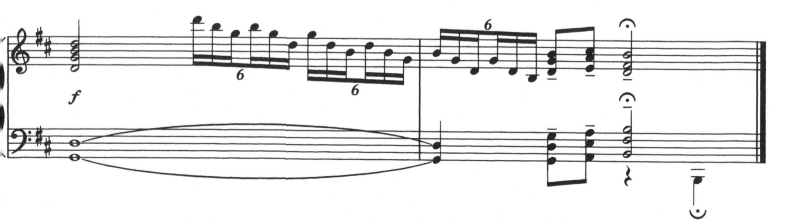

LISBON ANTIGUA
(In Old Lisbon)

English Lyric by HARRY DUPREE
Music by RAUL PORTELA, J. CALHARDO and A. do VALE
Arranged by DICK AVERRE

Latin beat, in two

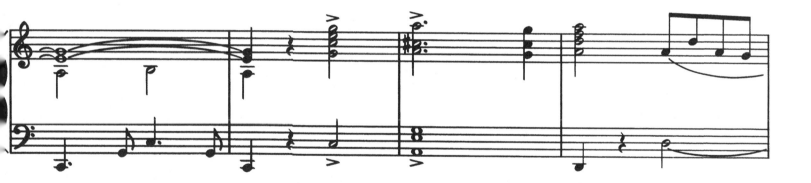

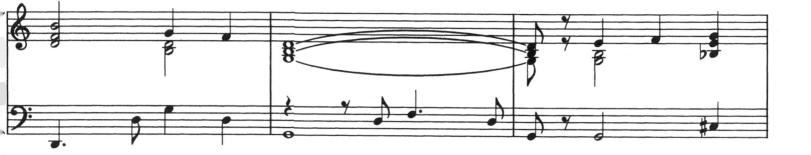

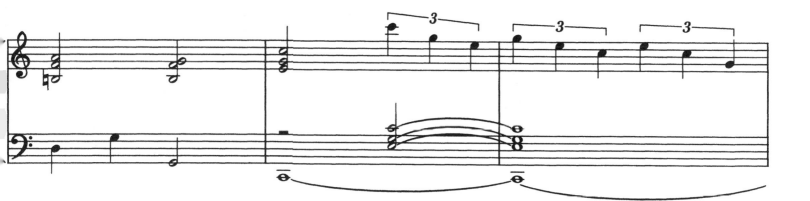

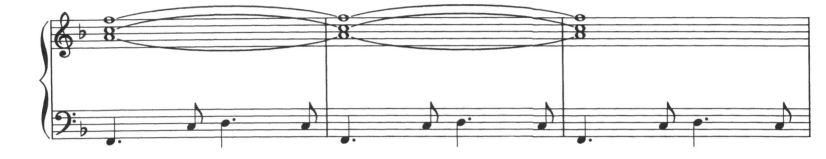

Freely

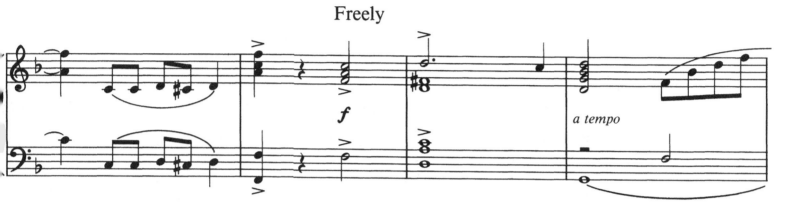

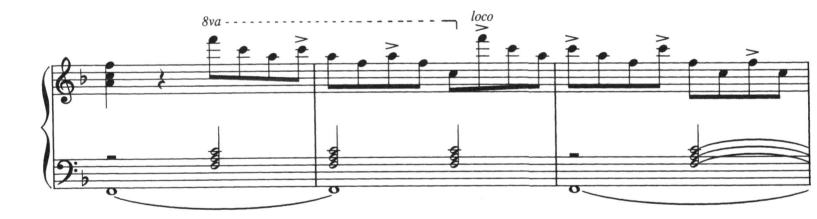

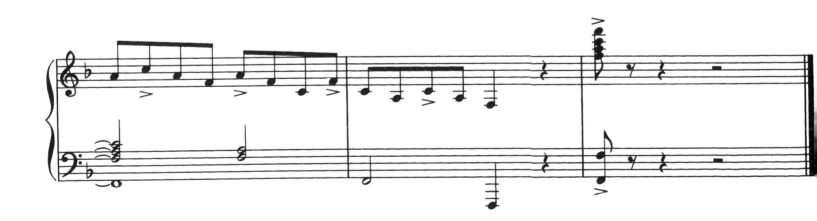

LOVE IS BLUE
(L'AMOUR EST BLEU)

English Lyric by BRYAN BLACKBURN
Original French Lyric by PIERRE COUR
Music by ANDRÉ POPP

THE POOR PEOPLE OF PARIS
(Joan's Song)

Original French words by RENE ROUZAUD
English words by JACK LAWRENCE
Music by MARQUERITE MONNOT
Arranged by DICK AVERRE

Moderately, delicately

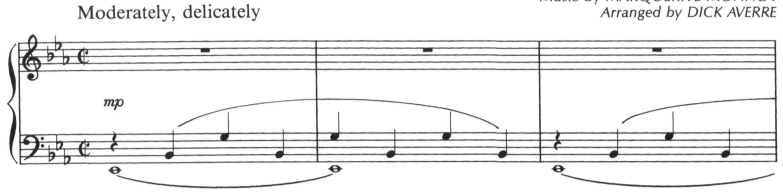

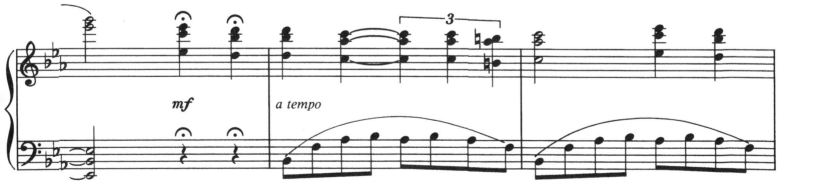

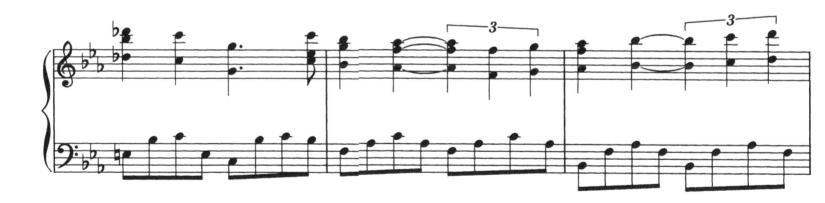

rall.

Somewhat slower

mp

simile

gradually slower

sub. f

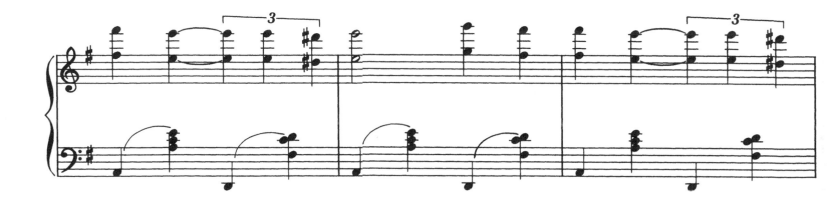

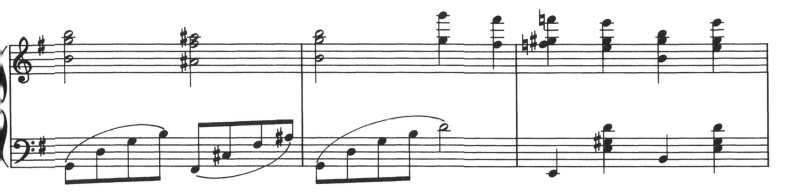

Slower

8va- - - - - -

gradually rit.

rit.

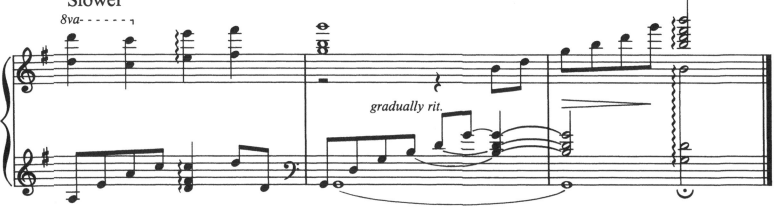

STRANGER ON THE SHORE

Words by ROBERT MELLIN
Music by ACKER BILK
Arranged by DICK AVERRE

Moderately, in a singing style

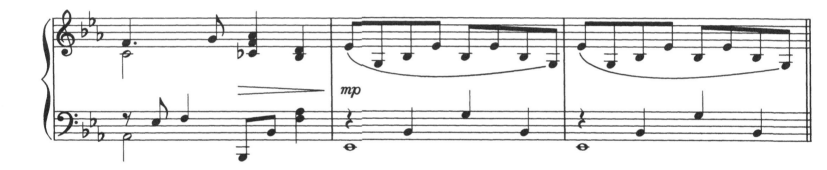

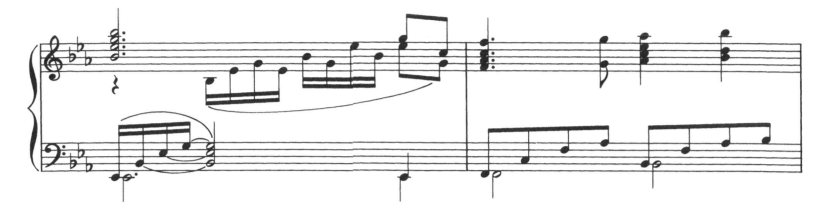

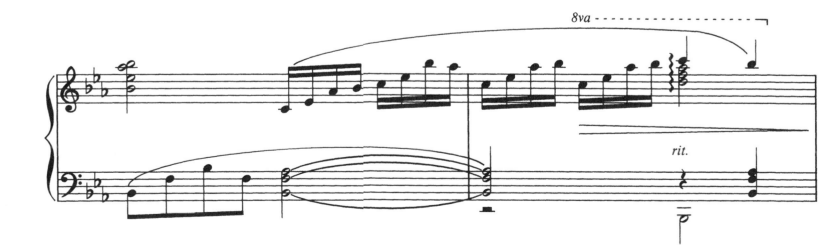

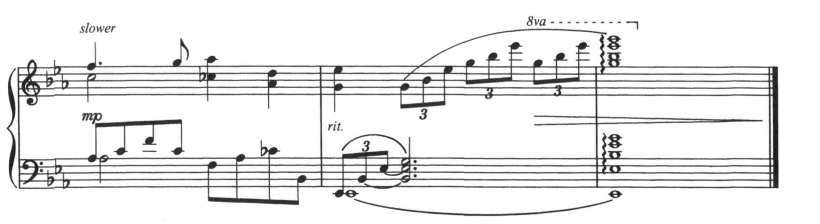

UNCHAINED MELODY

Words by HY ZARET
Music by ALEX NORTH
Arranged by DICK AVERRE

Moderately, in a singing style

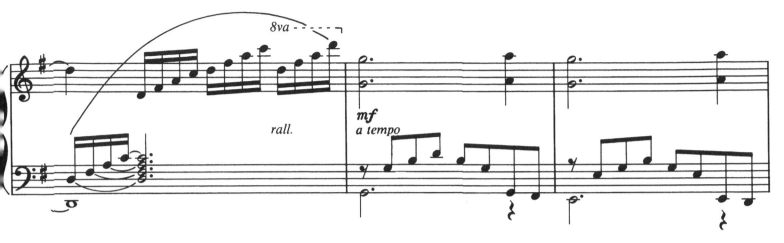

With motion (in two)

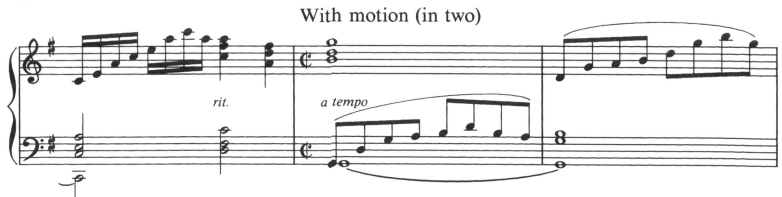

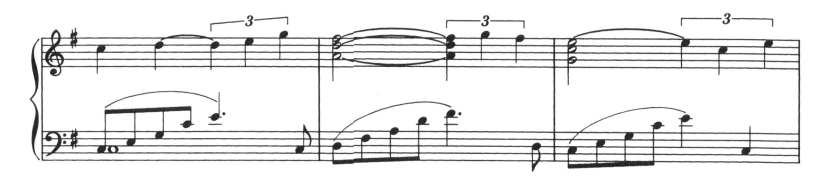

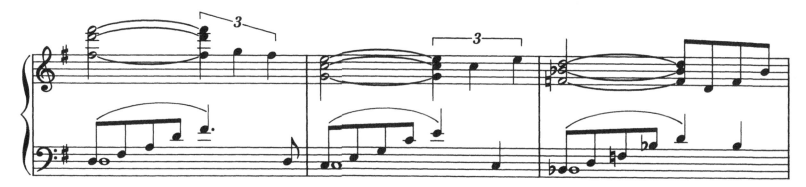

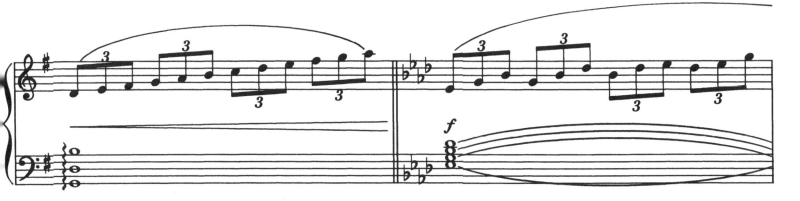

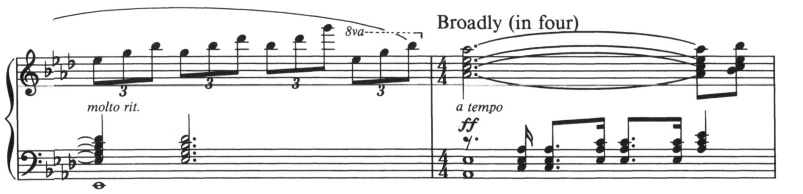

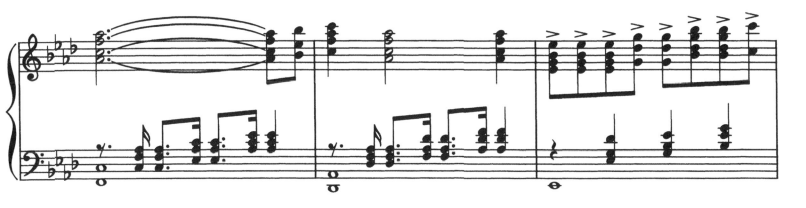

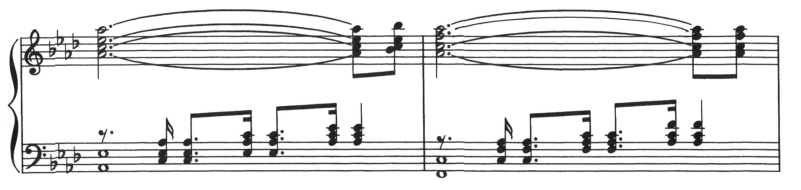

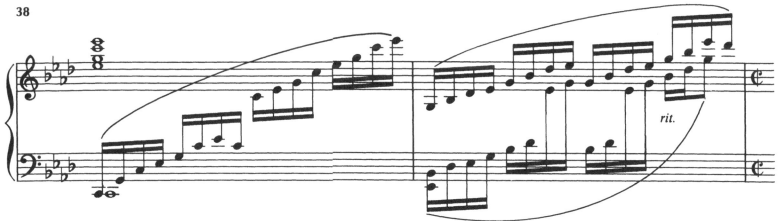

With motion (in two)

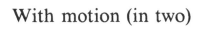

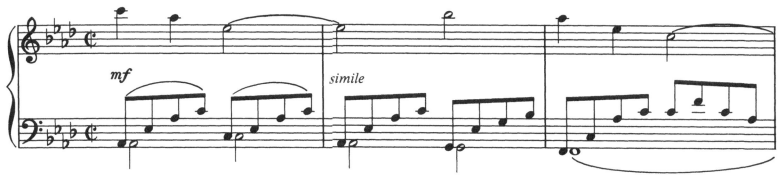

Agitated

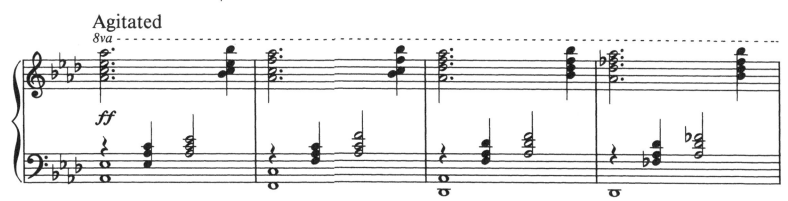

VOLARE
(Nel Blu, Depinto Di Blu)

English Lyric by MITCHELL PARISH
Original Italian Text by D. MODUGNO and F. MIGLIACCI
Music by DOMENICO MODUGNO
Arranged by DICK AVERRE

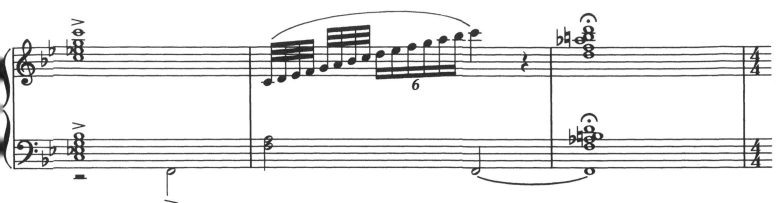

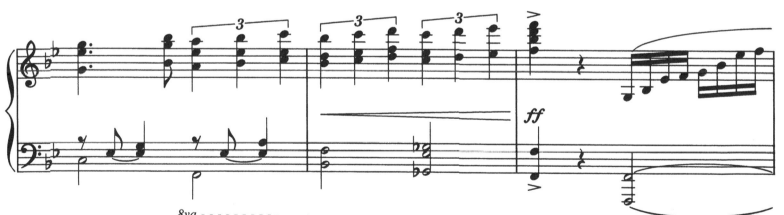

WONDERLAND BY NIGHT

Words by LINCOLN CHASE
Music by KLAUSS GUNTER-NEUMAN
Arranged by DICK AVERRE

Slowly and expressively

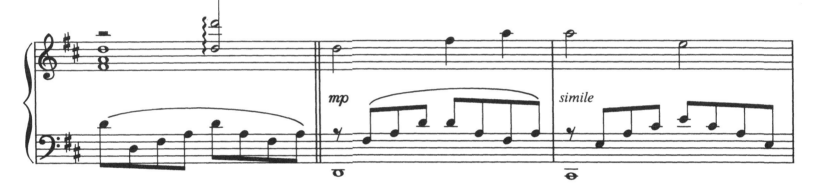

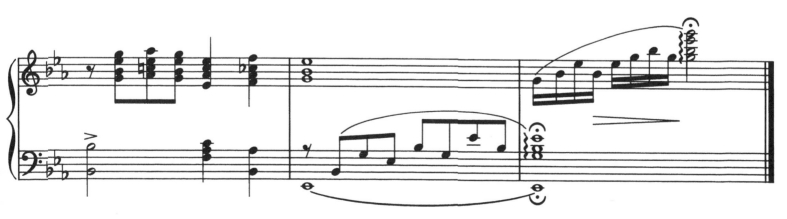